10-12

D0772640

ALASKA
wildlife portfolio

STEVEN NOURSE

Photography of Henry H. Holdsworth *and* Steven Nourse

FARCOUNTRY
PRESS

Dedications

I dedicate this book to the memory of my faithful golden retriever Denali.

Henry H. Holdsworth

I dedicate this book to my mother, who has encouraged and supported me to pursue my lifelong dreams of photography.

Steven Nourse

TITLE PAGE: Even bears need a good back rub now and then, as this bear did. Strange as it seems, the bear is resting against the tree after rubbing his back against it for nearly five minutes. STEVEN NOURSE

RIGHT: A flock of sandhill cranes flies past Mt. McKinley in Denali National Park. The sandbars along the McKinley River make excellent stopping points for the cranes on their annual migration between their nesting grounds in western Alaska and Siberia and their wintering range in Texas and New Mexico. HENRY H. HOLDSWORTH

ISBN: 1-56037-274-5

© 2004 Farcountry Press

Photography © by Henry H. Holdsworth and Steven Nourse.

For more information on our books write:

Farcountry Press, P.O. Box 5630,
Helena, Montana 59604;
call (800) 821-3874; or visit www.farcountrypress.com.

Created, produced, and designed in the United States.
Printed in Korea.

ALASKA, THE LAST FRONTIER—it is hard to think of this enormous state without visions of this phrase popping into your head. Like no other place in North America, Alaska is synonymous with thoughts of vast unexplored wilderness, untamed rivers, mysterious northern lights, and thundering glaciers. A land where unending herds of caribou still wander, where salmon choke the rivers and grizzly and polar bears rule. A place where you can leave civilization behind, where roads can get you only so far, and if you get out and explore you will probably be trekking across ground never before touched by human beings.

Everything about Alaska seems larger than life. The mountains are higher, moose taller, bears bigger, and tides more extreme. It is by far the largest U.S. state, at over twice the size of Texas. It is so spread out that, if a map of Alaska is superimposed over the lower 48 states, it reaches from coast to coast.

Alaska contains a dynamic range of ecosystems stretching from the rainforests of the southeast to the arctic tundra of the far north. But for all its size and beauty, its most amazing asset is the diversity of life that calls Alaska home. Its shores are home to whales and sea otters, its vast interior the realm of musk oxen and wolves, its snow-capped peaks the haven of Dall sheep and mountain goats, and its skies the domain of uncounted eagles. In Alaska you can witness the true meaning of the word "wilderness" and see in person the animals that bring that wilderness to life. One can spend a lifetime exploring this great land and barely scratch the surface of all it has to offer. It is my hope that the pages of this book will help shed some light on the private lives of Alaska's amazing wild inhabitants.

Henry H. Holdsworth

Eagle's Cathedral. A lone bald eagle flies through the Chilkat Bald Eagle Preserve at dawn to a backdrop of the Cathedral Peaks. From November to February, late-season salmon spawning in the Chilkat River Valley near Haines make it home to more than 3,000 eagles, the largest concentration in the world.
HENRY H. HOLDSWORTH

ALASKA IS A VAST, BREATHTAKING LAND that many amateur wildlife photographers dream about and professional photographers like Holdsworth and myself thrive on. This book is a collection of images created from our exciting treks to Alaska's coastline and ocean, tundra, lakes and rivers, mountains, and bush country. Here, patience and determination—along with luck and some knowledge—are needed to produce memorable photographs of animals in the wild.

Wildlife photography is often about knowing your subjects well enough to predict what might happen next. Being sensitive not to disturb your subject could mean missing a "perfect photo," but being insensitive could mean a mauling. Everyone knows Alaska is bear country, and if you travel extensively in the bush you will eventually meet this omnivore. Getting too close to a hidden moose calf is equally dangerous. A cow moose can turn a spring hike into an adrenaline-fueled hundred-yard dash.

Some of my most enjoyable times are on Alaska's 44,000 miles of shoreline. Freely exploring inlets, islands, and fiords from your own boat is a humbling and rewarding experience—one that can remind you of your small place in the world, whether caught in a violent storm, surrounded by whales, or beached from a huge wave generated by a calving glacier. But getting absorbed in the wonders around you is dangerous, too. I once lost control of my destiny while caught up in the beauty of harbor seals on an ice flow. Unaware of the snapping and crackling glacier ice surrounding me, I risked a puncture of my rubber inflatable boat that would quickly submerge me in the giant cocktail of icy water. Worse yet, the swirling currents were forcing me toward the hundred-foot, unstable wall of a tidewater glacier. I awoke to this situation in time to do something about it, but the lesson is clear: Witnessing the drama of life and death is part of the great Alaska experience—becoming part of it is not.

So, be aware of your surroundings by slowing down and carefully looking ahead and around you. This may keep both you and the wildlife safe and happy. You will also see more of the animals you came to see, and you may get that perfect photo as well.

Steven Nourse

Many of the photos in this book were taken from my home in Big Lake, Alaska. In order to photograph shy animals like these white-fronted geese I have a blind at my home. During migration these white-fronted geese stop only briefly at my home before heading to the Artic where they nest.
STEVEN NOURSE

RIGHT: A sow grizzly, with cubs in tow, fords the Brooks River in Katmai National Park. River crossings are one of many hazards young bears must endure. HENRY H. HOLDSWORTH

BELOW: A Dall sheep lamb tests its legs on Igloo Mountain in Denali National Park. These amazingly sure-footed animals use their climbing abilities to help protect themselves from the park's many predators. Spring is a wonderful time to witness Alaska's wild babies in action. HENRY H. HOLDSWORTH

During the autumn rut, exercise extreme care if you encounter a bull moose at close quarters. A fast retreat is usually the best response to these love-crazed animals. STEVEN NOURSE

The long-tailed jaeger spends most of the year at sea but comes to the tundra of Denali to nest. It is easily recognized by its long, streaming tail feathers. HENRY H. HOLDSWORTH

RIGHT: This sow and cub have no problem smelling the razor clams buried a foot under the hard-packed sand. The Alaska Peninsula west of Kodiak Island has fantastic scenery, great beach combing, and plenty of brown bears. STEVEN NOURSE

BELOW: A pika suns itself on the talus slopes of the Alaska Range. Unlike most small mammals found at high altitudes, the pika does not hibernate. It works steadily all summer drying grass in piles, which sustain it through Alaska's long snowy winter. HENRY H. HOLDSWORTH

ABOVE: The willow ptarmigan is the most widespread ptarmigan of Alaska, and thus suitably recognized as the state bird. This female is feeding on spring shoots, buds, insects, and flowers in Denali National Park. STEVEN NOURSE

FACING PAGE: The barren landscape north of the Arctic Circle is home to musk oxen. This solitary bull is roaming the colorful tundra north of the Brooks Range in search of cows of his own. STEVEN NOURSE

A common loon dashes across the water in an effort to take flight. The haunting call
of the loon is one of the most memorable sounds in nature. HENRY H. HOLDSWORTH

FACING PAGE: This long-tailed weasel investigates a bison skull in search of protein. Bison were reintroduced to Delta Junction from Montana to restore the indigenous animals that died out 500 years earlier. STEVEN NOURSE

BELOW: Herring gulls hitch a ride on an iceberg in Glacier Bay. HENRY H. HOLDSWORTH

ABOVE: A Savannah sparrow perches on lupine in western Alaska. This is just one of the 468 bird species that spend some portion of the year in the varied habitats of this huge state. HENRY H. HOLDSWORTH

FACING PAGE: Family portrait. A sow grizzly pauses with her yearling cubs on the tidal flats of the McNeil River State Game Sanctuary. Sedge grasses are an important food source for these coastal bears before the salmon runs of early summer. HENRY H. HOLDSWORTH

FOLLOWING PAGES: Humpbacks may be the whales most often sighted by visitors exploring southeast Alaska waterways. They sensibly seek the perfect waters by summering in Alaska and wintering in Hawaii. Here a humpback breeches in Stephens Passage near Admiralty Island. STEVEN NOURSE

ABOVE: A bald eagle spreads its wings in southeast Alaska. Bald eagles are a common sight in coastal Alaska, with an estimated 40,000 birds in the state. HENRY H. HOLDSWORTH

LEFT: Wolves are social mammals and howl to communicate to one another. The eerie sound can be as rewarding as a sighting itself. STEVEN NOURSE

FACING PAGE: Polychrome passage. A band of Dall sheep winds its way up the steep slopes of Polychrome Pass, in Denali National Park, to a rainbow backdrop over the Toklat River Valley. HENRY H. HOLDSWORTH

ABOVE: Red squirrels are found from southeast Alaska to the Brooks Range, where spruce cones make up the majority of their diet. They stay active year round, avoiding martens, owls, and other migratory birds of prey. STEVEN NOURSE

FACING PAGE: Harbor seals rest on an ice flow in Tracy Arm, southeast Alaska. In this area, the young are born on these frozen floating islands, and adults use them as resting spots when not feeding on the rich marine life in the depths below. STEVEN NOURSE

ABOVE: Blueberry bushes contribute to the arctic tundra's sassy red color in September. This dwarf shrub also provides grizzly bears with a valuable food source before denning. STEVEN NOURSE

FACING PAGE: Why does the number of caribou seem to fluctuate in Alaska? Is it because the delicate tundra takes years to regenerate? Is it wolf and bear predation? There is an old Alaskan saying: "No one knows the way of the wind or the caribou." STEVEN NOURSE

FACING PAGE: Male walruses bask in the sunshine on the rocky shores of Round Island in Bristol Bay, part of the Walrus Islands State Game Sanctuary in west-central Alaska. As many as 14,000 males use Round Island as a summer haul out (resting place) until the sea ice returns to the Bering Sea come winter. HENRY H. HOLDSWORTH

BELOW: The male walrus can be distinguished from females by his longer tusks. The tusks are used during mating battles with other males and as an aid when climbing on and off ice flows. HENRY H. HOLDSWORTH

Snowshoe hares change from grayish brown in the summer to almost pure white in winter. In years of delayed snowfall, these outcasts are easy prey to resident predators such as owls, eagles, foxes, and lynx. Early snow near the Alaska Range helps to camouflage this hare from the most common threats. STEVEN NOURSE

In late March when cabin fever has a grip on one's mind and body, the common redpoll breaks out in his breeding plumage, indicating to Alaskans that a long winter has ended. STEVEN NOURSE

ABOVE: Being the lowest on the food chain would make anybody nervous. A Richardson's ground squirrel in Denali lets out a chirp of alarm. STEVEN NOURSE

FACING PAGE: Eyes of a grizzly. A sow grizzly takes a moment to rest along the banks of the Brooks River in Katmai National Park. HENRY H. HOLDSWORTH

LEFT: Lily pads play an important role in the life of a red-necked grebe and her zebra-striped chicks. Both parents provide their young small fish, snails, and insects—all of which find shelter among these aquatic plants. STEVEN NOURSE

BELOW: Due to it's shortened larval period, the wood frog manages to survive as far north as the Brooks Range. This harmless amphibian sits near a poisonous fungi known as fly amanita or fly agaric. STEVEN NOURSE

RIGHT: "Jonathan Livingston Eagle" could easily be the name of this bald eagle as he soars with a flock of glaucous-winged gulls along the Kenai Coast. Eagles actually hunt seagulls when fish are scarce, as on this –27°F February morning. HENRY H. HOLDSWORTH

BELOW: A red fox takes advantage of a rare sunny day to get in an afternoon snooze. Foxes are a common sight on the mainland and many islands throughout Alaska. HENRY H. HOLDSWORTH

FACING PAGE: Bull caribou spar at the onset of the rutting season in early September. The fight for dominance helps ensure that the strongest genes are passed on to the next generation of caribou. HENRY H. HOLDSWORTH

BELOW: It didn't take this Denali road beaver long to find this broken down willow. Minutes before, a rutting bull moose stripped the limb from its cluster while removing velvet from his antlers. STEVEN NOURSE

Do other animals enjoy a special sunrise as much as people do? Although this Katmai brown bear has salmon on his mind, the sunrise colors surely demand his attention for a moment. STEVEN NOURSE

LEFT: My first encounter with musk oxen found me retreating through a willow thicket in the horizontal position, dreading the stomping that I anticipated and deserved. Apparently when I tripped and disappeared, the shaggy creature either was pleased with the outcome or did not feel like pursuing me through the tangle of brush.
STEVEN NOURSE

FACING PAGE: Thinking he is landing on a rock, a horned puffin drops in for an unexpected visit to a pair of male walruses.
HENRY H. HOLDSWORTH

RIGHT: A "snowbird" is a term Alaskans use to label a person who heads south when the snow, cold, and darkness encompass the state. These emperors certainly are among the few geese you could call Alaskan. They breed and nest in western Alaska and winter mainly in the Aleutian Islands, where this photo was taken. STEVEN NOURSE

BELOW: Mouth to mouth! Two young grizzlies do a little play fighting at the top of McNeil River Falls. When chum and silver salmon are running these falls from late June to mid-August, the McNeil River is transformed into a bear-viewing paradise. As many as 120 bears may fish this sanctuary's waters, and close to 70 bears may be seen at the falls at one time. HENRY H. HOLDSWORTH

Fishing near Brooks Lake is never without excitement, whether you're hooking world-class rainbow trout or avoiding brown bears that seem to be around every bend in the river. A sow and her spring cubs have successfully landed a sockeye salmon. As she faces a large male, she fears more for her cubs than for her slimy protein snack. STEVEN NOURSE

47

ABOVE: Looking for trouble. These young spring grizzly cubs keep a watchful eye out for other bears while their mother fishes for salmon along Mikfik Creek on the Alaska Peninsula. Adult male bears represent one of the biggest threats to cub survival. HENRY H. HOLDSWORTH

FACING PAGE: The short nights of summer make it a necessity for this great gray owl to hunt by day. This largest of North American owls stands more than 2 feet tall and is an inhabitant of the boreal and dense coniferous forests of southeast and central Alaska. HENRY H. HOLDSWORTH

LEFT: After a summer of solitude in the Denali high country, this bull moose searches for females in the valleys below. Moose are very vocal, and during peak mating activity in September both males and females can be heard. STEVEN NOURSE

BELOW: Red-backed voles are widely distributed around Alaska—in forests from Nome to Ketchikan. At night, this rodent will be sure to clean up any crumbs left by visitors in picnic areas. STEVEN NOURSE

ABOVE: Kissing puffins. Horned puffins in the part of their mating ritual known as billing. The isolated Pribilof Islands in the Bering Sea are an excellent destination for those wishing to see puffins and other seabirds up close. HENRY H. HOLDSWORTH

FACING PAGE: Bears of a feather stick together. This six-month-old Brooks River grizzly cub will stay close to its mom for two and a half years; then she leaves to start a new family. HENRY H. HOLDSWORTH

ABOVE: A hoary marmot lounges atop Polychrome Pass in Denali National Park, but he will spend most of the long days of summer foraging to build his fat reserves for a long winter of hibernation. HENRY H. HOLDSWORTH

FACING PAGE: As the summer ends and the colors of fall begin, these mature Dall rams will soon be testing each other to see who is king of the hill. In November and December, the sounds of crashing horns echo throughout the Alaska Range as summer companions battle during the annual rut. HENRY H. HOLDSWORTH

ABOVE: A black-legged kittiwake returns to the nest to tend to its young.
HENRY H. HOLDSWORTH

LEFT: The shear cliff walls of Round Island teem with new life. The
nutrient-rich oceans of the far north feed an abundant array of seabirds,
including the black-legged kittiwake, common murre, tufted and horned
puffins, pelagic cormorant, glaucous-winged gull, pigeon guillemot, and
parakeet auklet. Only 2 miles long and less than a mile wide, this small
steep island is home to some 250,000 nesting seabirds each summer.
HENRY H. HOLDSWORTH

ABOVE: Living in Alaska means living with wildlife. Each fall I am kept awake by a family of great horned owls screeching as the young venture out to become hunters. I photographed this owl perched on my deck from my bedroom. Photography from your bed.... It doesn't get any easier than that. STEVEN NOURSE

RIGHT: Serious combat between these unevenly matched bulls is unlikely. Both animals are well aware of their place in the hierarchy. Animals have a conserving nature about them; whether it's choosing their battles or their bedrooms, saving energy means survival. STEVEN NOURSE

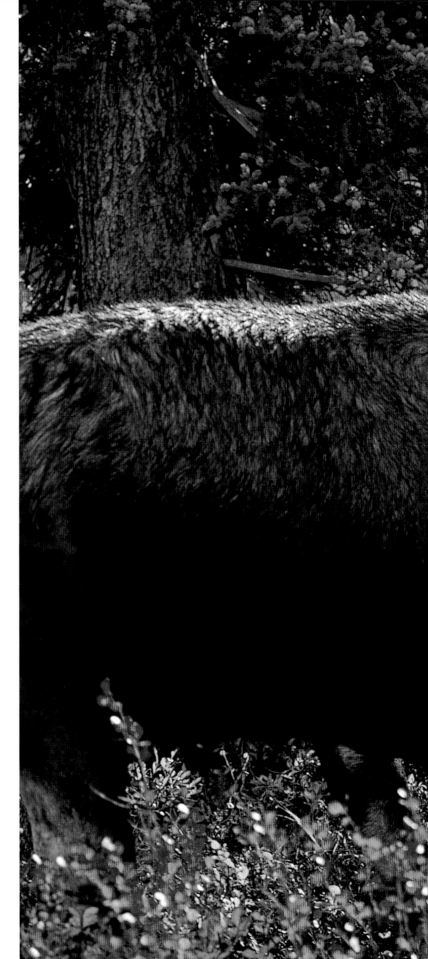

A sea otter bathes in late evening sun on Kachemak Bay near Homer. One of the most playful and fun-loving of all animals, the sea otter spends most of its life in the ocean, where it feeds on crabs, sea urchins, abalone, clams, and octopus. Unlike other marine mammals, the sea otter has no blubber but stays warm because of trapped air in its extremely dense fur. Once found throughout most of the North Pacific from northern Japan to the islands off southern California, they were hunted to near extinction by fur traders in the eighteen and nineteenth centuries. Though protected today by the federal Marine Mammal Protection Act, sea otters in Alaska are still threatened by oil spills.

HENRY H. HOLDSWORTH

ABOVE: Except for a few nurtured trees planted from the mainland, the Aleutian Islands are barren of green lofty perches. Without traveling over 1,000 miles, this immature bald eagle will have to settle for rocks and clefts, or soar on the relentless wind that batters the islands. STEVEN NOURSE

FACING PAGE: A cow moose enjoys a meal of succulent aquatic vegetation in Wonder Lake. Moose can generally be found in the vicinity of fresh water, which helps them to stay cool and avoid insects in the summer months. HENRY H. HOLDSWORTH

LEFT: Brightly colored starfish line a tidepool on Barnoff Island near Sitka. HENRY H. HOLDSWORTH

BELOW: A golden-crowned sparrow sings from a lichen-covered rock in Bristol Bay. HENRY H. HOLDSWORTH

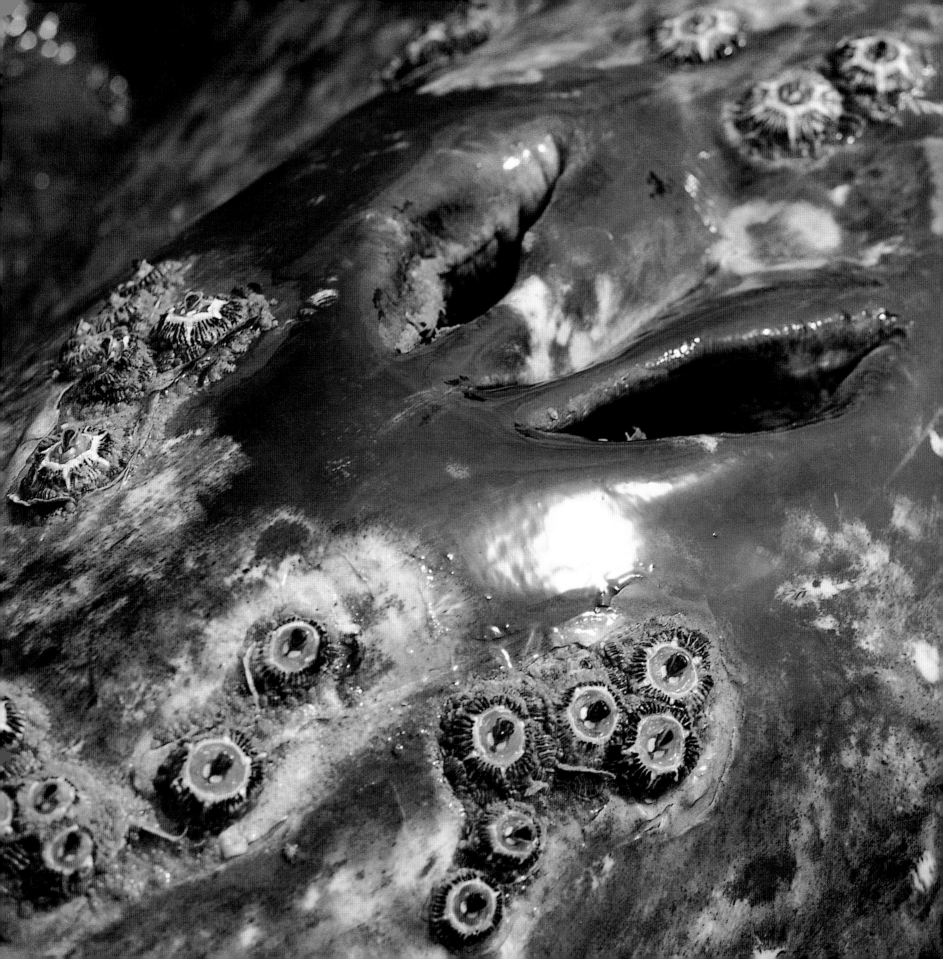

ABOVE AND FACING PAGE: Barnacles take a free ride on the back of a gray whale. Each year these massive creatures travel from mating and calving grounds in Baja, Mexico, where this calf was born, to summer feeding grounds in the Bering and Chuckchi Seas in northern Alaska—one of the longest migrations of any mammal, covering 10,000–14,000 miles roundtrip and taking two or three months in each direction. HENRY H. HOLDSWORTH

FACING PAGE: Born in the depths of winter, a pair of two-month-old polar bear cubs emerge from the den with their mother. They will follow her for their first two or three years as she hunts seals on the arctic ice. Polar bears are superbly adapted to life in the far north, with thick, hollow hair and massive paws that aid in swimming. They are the world's largest land predators, with adult males weighing 750–1,500 pounds. HENRY H. HOLDSWORTH

BELOW: The change from summer brown to winter white feathers helps this ptarmigan blend into its surroundings. HENRY H. HOLDSWORTH

RIGHT: Low clouds and Chugach Mountains set the backdrop for these Canada geese. Anchorage's well-fertilized lawns and lack of predators have encouraged geese to take up residence there. Several years ago, a crew of airmen lost their lives when their plane collided with a flock of geese. STEVEN NOURSE

BELOW: Aptly named, a willow ptarmigan peeks out from willows in bright autumn color. HENRY H. HOLDSWORTH

ABOVE: There may be no better photo opportunity than a calm after a storm. This redpoll was enjoying the sun's warmth when a gust of wind landed a reminder of the previous night on its head. STEVEN NOURSE

RIGHT: Musk oxen were eliminated from Alaska in the mid-1800s and reintroduced from Greenland in the 1930s. They now thrive in this inhospitable landscape. A trip north of the Brooks Range on the James Dalton Highway can reveal a glimpse of these prehistoric-looking animals. STEVEN NOURSE

LEFT: A grizzly bear snags a bright-red sockeye salmon in September. As the sockeye turn from silver to red, spawn, and then near the end of their lifespan, they provide a valuable food source for bears fattening up for a long winter's nap. HENRY H. HOLDSWORTH

BELOW: By mid-August, sockeye or red salmon are reaching their spawning ground in Big Lake, Alaska. A viewing area and park southeast of Big Lake gives visitors an opportunity to see this fight for life. STEVEN NOURSE

ABOVE: The black-capped chickadee is a welcome visitor on a cold winter morning. Full of energy and oblivious to the frigid ice, this inquisitive year-round resident brightens a dark, dreary day. STEVEN NOURSE

FACING PAGE: As September snow flies, a flock of willow ptarmigan are halfway through their change from summer brown to winter white. STEVEN NOURSE

LEFT: A lone Dall ram surveys his domain high in the Alaska Range. Denali National Park was established in 1917 mainly to protect these majestic high-country dwellers.
STEVEN NOURSE

BELOW: A pair of baby hoary marmots keep a wary eye out for golden eagles, foxes, and wolves. HENRY H. HOLDSWORTH

Before dawn, a large male grizzly ambles down the shoreline of Naknek Lake in Katmai National Park. Scenes such as this have been played out for thousands of years and take one back to a time when humans were much closer to the natural world. To witness events such as this one and make time stand still are what make a visit to Alaska the trip of a lifetime. HENRY H. HOLDSWORTH

ABOVE: After a sudden downpour, these thirsty Richardson's ground squirrels emerge from their burrows to lick trapped water droplets from a dwarf fireweed plant. STEVEN NOURSE

FACING PAGE: Sitka black-tailed deer are numerous on islands in and around southeast Alaska. They now flourish around the Prince William Sound and on Kodiak and Afognak Islands because of transplantation. Recent sightings nearer Anchorage have excited hunters and disappointed gardeners. STEVEN NOURSE

ABOVE: Common murres nest together on shallow ledges. Their eggs are oblong, so if they roll they go in a circle instead of falling off the cliff. HENRY H. HOLDSWORTH

FACING PAGE: Whales generally rise to the surface several times consecutively to breathe and then sound, or dive deeply. This humpback whale is sounding to release air bubbles in a circle that will confuse and concentrate its prey, a technique known as bubble net feeding. STEVEN NOURSE

LEFT: It's always a special feeling when wildlife trusts you enough to introduce their young ones to you. On a fall day in Denali, this beaver family swam within several feet of me, communicating with soft purrs to one another. STEVEN NOURSE

RIGHT: We all need a place to live and raise our young. An apartment now sits on the location where this Canada goose chose to nest and raise her young last year. STEVEN NOURSE

BELOW: The red fox has three color phases, with rusty orange being the most common and this black color morph the rarest. The cross fox is a combination of these two, with a rusty gray body and a black back and forelegs. STEVEN NOURSE

RIGHT: Katmai National Park has spectacular scenery and safe wildlife viewing. With the guidance of rangers and the protection of elevated viewing platforms, Katmai has a commendable safety record. STEVEN NOURSE

BELOW: More than two hundred islands, stretching over 1,000 miles from mainland Alaska toward southern Russia, make up the Aleutian Chain. These treeless islands are home to many bald eagles, who make their ground nests near cliff edges, discouraging foxes brought by people for fur farming decades ago. STEVEN NOURSE

ABOVE: National parks are effective places to see and photograph wolves because of the lifelong protection they receive there. The next best place is a remote area in the winter near a food source; a winterkill moose near Bethal attracted a pack of six, not to mention numerous foxes and a wolverine. STEVEN NOURSE

RIGHT: A place of solitude, this is the Alaska I love. At deep sub-zero temperatures, an extreme appreciation for life exists. Denali's 20,320-foot peak looms in the background while morning rays bathe the Alaska Range in an alpine glow too rich for words. It's a time to reflect where you are going and where you have been. STEVEN NOURSE

ABOVE: All dressed up and nowhere to go. Horned puffins decorate a lichen-covered rock in Bristol Bay. Puffin viewing can be the highlight of any voyage on the waters of coastal Alaska.
HENRY H. HOLDSWORTH

FACING PAGE: Mallards in motion—a slow shutter speed and unique angle captured the motion of these mallard ducks in a swift river current.
STEVEN NOURSE

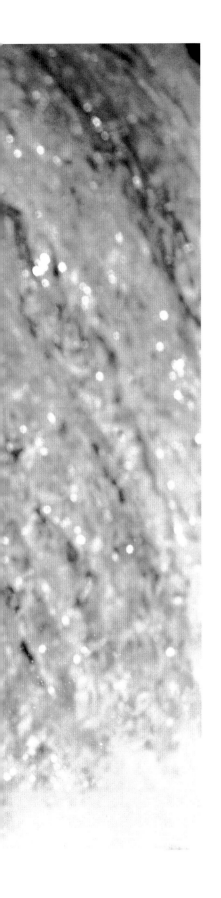

LEFT: Guess who's coming to dinner? A coastal grizzly anticipates its next meal of sockeye salmon at Brooks River Falls in Katmai National Park. An adult bear may consume sixty fish a day during the height of the salmon run. HENRY H. HOLDSWORTH

BELOW: Grizzly tracks mark the crossing of a bear on the tidal flats of the McNeil River State Game Sanctuary. HENRY H. HOLDSWORTH

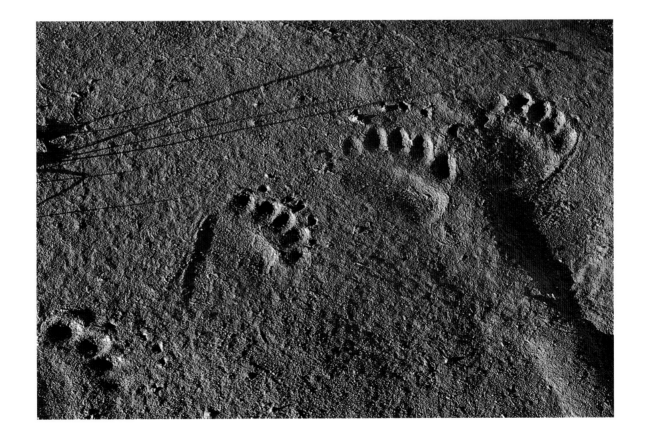

FACING PAGE: Nothing can make a strenuous climb more rewarding than the company of the docile Dall sheep. Sitting among these pure-white majestic mammals will certainly be part of the Alaska stories you will cherish for many years. STEVEN NOURSE

BELOW: Some brown bears fish at Anan Creek near Wrangell, but black bears are the predominate users of this resource. STEVEN NOURSE

FACING PAGE: Animals definitely have individual personalities. Every once in a while you meet that special one. This bald eagle was one tough cookie. If it wasn't her huge size that intimidated her peers, it was her ferocious attitude. STEVEN NOURSE

BELOW: A shy and solitary member of the weasel family, the wolverine is a cunning and powerful animal. This wolverine has come upon a piece of moose hide in the Arctic National Wildlife Refuge. STEVEN KAZLOWSKI

Stellar sea lions haul out on North Marble Island in Glacier Bay National Park and Preserve. Glacier Bay is one of the true natural wonders of Alaska, supporting a vast array of marine mammals, bears, and birds. On a clear day the backdrop of thundering glaciers and the 15,000-foot peaks of the Fairweather Range are breathtaking. This amazing park has been recognized internationally as both a World Heritage Site and a Biosphere Reserve. HENRY H. HOLDSWORTH

ABOVE: A pair of trumpeter swans fly out of the clouds surrounding the Chilkat Mountains nears Haines. Trumpeters mate for life and nest on the ponds and lakes Alaska's interior. They may winter as far south as the Columbia River in Washington state. HENRY H. HOLDSWORTH

FACING PAGE: Coyote numbers seem to be steadily growing in Alaska and especially around Anchorage, where the courageous critters take advantage of unlimited meal opportunities. This canine was searching for waterfowl after Valdez suffered from an extreme overnight blizzard. STEVEN NOURSE

LEFT: A trio of black oyster catchers strut their stuff during mating season at Glacier Bay National Monument. With glaciers looming in the background, spring birding in Alaska is something not to be missed. HENRY H. HOLSWORTH

BELOW: The pelagic cormorant is one of three cormorant species to nest on Alaska's rocky sea cliffs. The red-faced and double-crested cormorants are seen here as well. HENRY H. HOLDSWORTH

Fall and winter stresses can be tremendous for the moose. Deep snows force animals to locations where feeding and traveling is easier. These antlerless bull moose find refuge in a streambed south of the Alaska Range. STEVEN NOURSE

ABOVE: The Northern hawk owl is the most diurnal of all North American owls. This species has adapted to the endless amount of daylight of northern summers. It can be seen hunting in clearings near boreal forest at any time of the day. STEVEN NOURSE

FACING PAGE: In the past, wolves were persecuted to near annihilation. Recent human culling activities, such as programs that benefit moose and caribou populations by hunting the wolves from the air, have caused the wolves to become even more elusive and secretive. STEVEN NOURSE

ABOVE: A curious red fox kit takes a cautious peek out of the den. HENRY H. HOLDSWORTH

FACING PAGE: Trumpeter swans feed before heading to their wintering quarters farther south. STEVEN NOURSE

Fall colors add a majestic backdrop as this grizzly surveys fishing grounds at the mouth of the Brooks River on the Alaska Peninsula. HENRY H. HOLDSWORTH

LEFT. A newborn ptarmigan chick tries to camouflage itself amid tundra wildflowers.
HENRY H. HOLDSWORTH

FACING PAGE: It is a myth that porcupines shoot quills. When frightened, they actually swing their tail in an attempt to stick the barbed quills into an adversary.
STEVEN NOURSE

ABOVE: A wintering Dall ewe poses in front of frost-laden branches on a sub-zero day in Canada's Kluane National Park. Sheep Mountain is an excellent place to view Dall sheep for those heading up the Alaska Highway. Kluane is northwest of Haines Junction in the Yukon Territory. HENRY H. HOLDSWORTH

FACING PAGE: A boreal owl finds shelter from the wind behind the trunk of an aspen tree. This common but seldom-seen resident of the boreal forest inhabits much of the central part of the state as far west as King Salmon on the Alaska Peninsula. An adult bird stands only 10 inches tall. HENRY H. HOLDSWORTH

LEFT: Being a greenhorn (cheechako) to Alaska, I have made many foolish mistakes. I once found what I thought was a great floating anchorage for the Zodiac I was living on—until I saw another piece of ice roll, revealing its enormous house-size mass. Lesson: If you can't fly like these gulls, stay away from the ice. STEVEN NOURSE

BELOW: An Arctic tern calls out to its mate. These terns spend most of their life in the air, flying from breeding grounds in the Arctic to their winter home at the edge of Antarctica. They travel some 22,000 miles each year, roughly the circumference of the earth—the longest migration of any bird. HENRY H. HOLDSWORTH

On the tundra where trees are in short supply, this signpost makes an excellent chin-scratcher for a female grizzly. Sabal Pass is one of the best areas to view bears in Denali National Park.

HENRY H. HOLDSWORTH